31 Days
Of Prayer

31 DAYS
Of PRAYER

Miracles, Signs, and Wonders

CHARLENE LA-TRELL BROWN

XULON PRESS

Xulon Press
2301 Lucien Way #415
Maitland, FL 32751
407.339.4217
www.xulonpress.com

Paperback ISBN-13: 978-1-66281-659-8
Ebook ISBN-13: 978-1-66281-660-4

1 Thessalonians 5:17 NKJV
Pray without Ceasing.

1 Timothy 2:5 NKJV
For there is one GOD, and one mediator between GOD and men, the Man Christ JESUS.

TABLE OF CONTENTS

SUBMISSION

LORD I want to Thank You,

For allowing me to see another beautiful day filled with Your glory. I come with my hands up surrendering myself to You. I ask that You have Your way in my life, O GOD. I Love you LORD, with my whole heart and I give You all the praise, glory, and honor. Lord, remove anything that is in, on, or around me that is not of You now. I want to be pleasing and acceptable in Your glorious sight JESUS. LORD, continue to order my steps and make every crooked path straight. LORD, I ask that You create in me a clean heart and renew a right spirit within me. Have Your way in my life O Lord GOD. In JESUS's name, I pray. Amen.

Psalm 51:10-13 NKJV Create in me a clean heart, O God, and renew a steadfast spirit within me. Do not cast me away from your presence, and do not take your Holy spirit from me. Restore to me the joy of your salvation; and uphold me by your generous spirit. Then will I teach transgressors your ways, and sinners shall be converted to you.

DELIVERANCE

Heavenly Father,

I come to You now God, giving You all of me, with lifted hands and an open heart to receive the blessings from You. Heavenly Father, I come to You on bended knees for You to deliver me from anything that has me bound and captive; anything or anyone that is keeping me from You. I ask, Father, that You break soulties, emotional soul-ties, generational curses, strongholds or evil words that were spoken over me, and everything that was sent by the enemy. Heavenly Father, I ask God that You deliver and set me free now, in the name of Jesus, from any addictions, bad habits, and wrongful thinking, in the name of Jesus. LORD, Your Word says that I ask, and I shall receive, seek and I shall find, knock and it shall be opened unto me, so God, I'm asking, seeking, and knocking as You are the only one that can do it in the mighty name of Jesus! I speak to anything that is in my life, as a hindrance, barrier, and barricade that it is cancelled, removed, and destroyed and thrown into the Lake of Fire now in Jesus's name! I pray, God, and thank you for releasing me in Jesus's name, I pray. AMEN, AMEN, and AMEN.

Galatians 5:1 NKJV Stand fast therefore in the liberty by which Christ has made us free, and do not be entangled again by the yoke of bondage.

Psalm 34:17 NKJV The righteous cry out, and the LORD hears; and he delivers them out all their troubles.

OBEDIENCE

Dear Lord,

I come humbly before You with praise and thanksgiving, surrendering my all to You. I want to thank you for Your grace and mercy that You have placed upon my life to glorify You. LORD, I give You my desires for Your will for my life because You always know what is best for me. My desire is to be obedient unto You and to please You. Lord, I ask for Your help and strength to do what You need me to do and not man, for You said that You will never leave me nor forsake me. I thank you LORD in advance because it's already done in JESUS's name, I pray. AMEN, AMEN, and AMEN.

John 14:15 NKJV If you love me, keep my commandments.

Luke 11:28 NKJV But He said, 'More than that, blessed are those who hear the word of God and keep it!"

FAITH

Believing JESUS even when you cannot see what you are hoping for.

Dear LORD JESUS,

Thank you for this beautiful day filled with Your faithfulness. Thank you for Your miracles, signs, and wonders that only You can perform. Thank you for Your grace and mercy that are anew every morning.

LORD, help me when I feel weak and over-whelmed; give me Your peace that surpasses all understanding. Lord, remove anything that is not of You and release me into Your glorious presence, endowing me with all of You. LORD, release Your angels to minister and war on my behalf. In JESUS's name, I thank you and pray. Amen, Amen, and Amen.

2 Corinthians 5:7 NKJV For we walk by Faith, not by sight.

NIGHTY PRAYER

Dear GOD

Thank you for allowing me to be kept by You. Your word says that He that keeps you does not slumber nor sleep. Thank you for Your hedge of protection, for You are my strong tower and I can run to You for safety. Thank you for eternal life, which is pleasing and acceptable in Your sight, O LORD, my rock and my redeemer. Father, I thank you for healing my body, mind, and soul. By Your stripes, I am healed, delivered, and set free. According to Your Word, John 8:36, "So if the SON sets you free, you will be free indeed." I want to thank you for giving me the desires of my heart, because You have placed them there. Guard my heart LORD GOD in JESUS's name, I pray. AMEN, AMEN, and AMEN.

THANKSGIVING

Dear JESUS,

I want to take this precious time to thank you for allowing me to see another day of Your immaculate glory. Thank you for the hedge of Your awesome protection from the hands of the evil one. I thank you for the godly relationships and divine assignments You have ordained in my life. I am so thankful for Your eyes that are placed upon me that allows me to be a witness of Your power, peace, and loving kindness. Lord, I thank you for allowing me to see and experience life through Your eyes. I pray that You will allow me to continue to love, speak, walk, talk, and to pray, as You have called me to do. In JESUS's name, I pray. AMEN, AMEN, and AMEN.

1 Thessalonians 5:18 NKJV In everything give thanks; for this is the will of GOD in Christ JESUS for you.

The Angel of the LORD has come to help and assist you with everything you need.

More peace, understanding, and awakening of your Spirit.

I AM HERE SAID THE LORD OF HOST... I AM HERE TO HELP YOU.

I CAME TO GIVE YOU LIFE MORE ABOUNTANTLY.

GUIDANCE

Dear JESUS,

Lord, I thank you for choosing and loving me. I want to thank you for the supernatural gift of life that is only by the power of Your almighty hand. Thank you for forgiving me and my sins, Father, and for loving me more than I will ever know. Lord, show me what is in my way, and give me the strength to push through and remove any entanglements. Teach me Your precepts, GOD, and order my steps. Lord, change my name on today and give me the land that You want me to possess. I am thankful for Your angels that minister and war in the spirit and natural realms on my behalf. I ask that You make every crooked place straight and lead me into Your righteousness. I give You all the glory and honor, O LORD!

Thank you, GOD, for your servants in JESUS's name, I pray and receive. Amen.

Psalm 32:8 NKJV I will instruct you and teach you in the way you should go; I will guide you with My eye.

ANGELIC ACTIVITY

Hebrews 1:14 NKJV Are they not all ministering spirits sent forth to minister for those who will inherit salvation?

Psalm 91:11 NKJV For He shall give His Angels charge over you, to keep you in all your ways.

Hebrews 13:2 NKJV Do not forget to entertain strangers, for by so doing some have unwittingly entertained angels.

Dear Father,

I'm so grateful to be called into your light that changed my life in every area. Thank you for the spiritual gifts to see and hear from You as being a witness of the Gospel of Jesus Christ. Thank you for Your angels that minister and war on my behalf, as they are real and assist me daily. I pray that every angel that is being held up by any dark force will break the darkness of evil and send their angels to assist for the manifestations of your will to be released here on the earth in Jesus's name, I pray. Amen.

POWER

Acts 1:8 NKJV But you shall receive power, when the Holy Spirit has come upon you: and you shall be witnesses to Me in Jerusalem, and in all Judea, and in Samaria, and to the end of the earth.

1Corinthians 6:14
NKJV And God both raised up the Lord and will also raise us up by His power.

Dear Lord,

I want to thank you for having ALL power in Your hands, for nothing is too hard for You. LORD, you are strong and mighty, and I ask that You open my eyes to see You move in my life. In the beginning, You spoke the word and it was so; let there be light and it was. I want to thank you for Your Holy Spirit that's inside of me to allow me to speak Your word and to bear witness of Your POWER. You are everything and You are everywhere. You can go where I cannot, and I thank you for being awesome.

I thank you for raising me up, Lord, in JESUS's name, I pray. AMEN, Amen, and Amen.

GOODNESS

Dear Heavenly Father,

I thank you for being my everything; for allowing me to see another day and seeing Your miraculous miracles every moment. Lord GOD, I thank you for Your creations that are wonderfully and beautiful made. I thank you for showing me Your joy that is everlasting. I ask that You position my heart, mind, spirit, and everything that is concerning me to manifest. I want to take time to thank you for Your glory and impartation, in JESUS's name, I pray. Amen.

Psalm 145:5-7 NKJV I will meditate on the glorious splendor of your majesty, And on Your wonderous works. Men shall speak of the might of your awesome acts, And I will declare Your greatness. They shall utter the memory of your great goodness And shall sing of your righteousness.

STRENGTH

Dear Heavenly Father,

I want to thank you for another day in Your court; another day to witness the greatness of You and Your presence. LORD, remove anything that is not of You and Your perfect will for my life. Lord, order my steps to bring me into the complete alignment of You and Your Word. Thank you, LORD GOD, for Your strength, for I cannot do anything on my own without You. For You are the creator of heaven and earth, giving me peace that surpasses all understanding. LORD, I thank you for the gift of discernment and every spiritual gift. I ask that You activate my words of encouragement and prayer to be a blessing to others. Guide my steps, for they are ordered by You. I ask that You give me wise counsel, so I can answer everyone accordingly to your will In Jesus's mighty name, I pray. Amen.

I LOVE YOU, LORD JESUS!

Nehemiah 8:10 NKJV Then he said to them, Go your way, eat the fat, and drink the sweet, and send portions to those for whom nothing is prepared, For this day is holy to the LORD: Do not sorrow, for the Joy of the LORD is your strength.

RESPONSES

Dear Heavenly Father,

Thank you for loving and taking great care of me, forgiving my sins, and leading me into the paths of righteousness for Your namesake. Lord, I ask that You speak and be the door to my lips, allowing every response be Your response. Let me answer every man accordingly in JESUS's name. Remove anything and anyone that is a hinderance to my destiny You have planned for my life. Increase my faith to Your capacity and shine forth Your marvelous light in my life to bring You glory in JESUS's name, I pray, Lord, Amen.

Colossians 4:6 NKJV Let your speech always be with grace, seasoned with salt, that you may know how you ought to answer each one.

LOVE

Dear GOD,

Thank you for Your perfect love that means everything to me. Thank you for being the perfect father who knew me before I was in my mother's womb. Lord, I want to thank you for Your guidance and commandments that are the manual and blueprint for my life. I thank you for Your son JESUS, who laid down His life and paid the price for us all. Teach me Your ways, O GOD, so I can love like You in Jesus's name, I pray. Amen, Amen, and Amen.

1 John 4:18 NKJV There is no fear in love but perfect love casts out fear, because fear involves torment., But he who fears has not been made perfect in love.

FORGIVENESS

Dear Heavenly Father

I thank you for all You have done, did, and are doing for me and my family. I am so grateful and thankful for You, Lord. Lord, help me to forgive others without a second thought. Your Word says that I must forgive, because You first forgave me. Nothing or no one is bigger than You. My desire is to be more like You, Jesus, in every minute of this life. I thank you for forgiving me and placing me on the right path, as you are guarding my heart. In Jesus's name, I pray. Amen.

Ephesians 4:32 NKJV And be kind to one another, tenderhearted, forgiving one another, even as God in Christ forgave you.

FRIENDS

Dear GOD,

You know my heart and desire to please You instead of man. Lord, I ask that You send the ones who you have assigned to my destiny and to fulfil Your purpose. Help me to be the friend that loves at all times and not to live in offence, for we wrestle not against flesh and blood. I thank you for the friends You have placed in my life and for the new ones to come in this next chapter. I want to thank you for being my friend first, leading the way, light, and truth. I ask that You mature me and teach me to be a better friend. In Jesus's name, I pray. Amen.

Proverbs 27:17 NKJV As iron sharpens iron. so, a man sharpens the countenance of his friend.

John 15:13 NKJV Greater love has no one than this, than to lay down one's life for his friends.

ACCEPTANCE

Dear Jesus,

I thank you for adopting me into Your royal priesthood. Thank you for writing my name into the Book of Life. Lord, I thank you for changing my name, address, and life according to Your perfect will. Thank you for loving and taking great care of me, allowing my family and I to have an inheritance that is eternal. I ask that You continue to bless and keep us to speak, love, and walk like You. I want to thank you with all my heart for being the good shepherd (for I lack nothing) in Jesus's name, I pray. Amen.

SUPERNATURAL HEALING

Dear Heavenly Father,

I want to thank you for allowing me to wake up to be a part of this day, filled with everything from You. Thank you, Jesus, for Your sweet grace and mercy that are anew every morning. Father God, I ask that You cleanse and wash me in Your precious blood, creating in me a clean heart of flesh. Lord, please remove anything in my body that is not of Your nature and pour Your loving Holy Spirit in me that flows, keeps, heals, delivers, and restores me back to my youth, O Lord, for Your lovingkindness. I ask that You bring forth the sudden transformation of my mind, body, and soul from the inside, Lord. I need a supernatural healing and a powerful touch from You. Lord, allow me to drink from Your living well that never runs dry. I thank you for the strong faith that moves mountains. I speak to every mountain of doubt, fear, loneliness, sickness, mediocracy, stagnation, procrastination, poverty, doublemindness, stubbornness, stiff neck, disobedient, and rejection in the name of Jesus to be removed and casted into the sea. Lord, I ask that You pour out an overflow of Your spirit and make me new, because You have created me in Your image. I am healed, delivered, and set free from all evil things in Jesus's name, I pray. Amen.

Jeremiah 30:17 NKJV For I will restore health to you and heal you of your wounds, says the LORD, because they called you an outcast saying: "This is Zion; No one seeks her."

MY PRAYER LIFE

Dear Heavenly Father,

I want to thank you with everything in me to bow down and praise Your holy name. I thank you for prayer that allows me to personally communicate with You in peace and confidence, because You are worthy. I trust You, Lord, in every situation because You have never failed me, nor let me down. Every word of Yours is true, and You are not a man that You should lie nor the son of man that should repent. I can call on You in the late midnight hour and at any giving moment, and You always come to my rescue. I thank you for filling me with the Holy Spirit that helps me to pray when I do not know what to pray for. Thank you for the gift of intercession to be able to be sensitive to the Holy Spirit, while standing in the gap and praying for others. According to Your Word, I can/will seek You early in the morning and You can be found. Heavenly Father, I ask that You take me to a place to seek You deeper and diligently. I can't thank you enough for being here for me and loving me unconditionally, giving me the keys to Your royal kingdom. You always make ways out of no ways; in Jesus's name, I pray. Amen.

Colossians 4:2 NKJV Continue earnestly in prayer, being vigilant in it with thanksgiving.

LEADERS

Dear Jesus,

I thank you for your examples of leadership and leaders. Lord, I ask that I will always be in the company of Your called and chosen ones, which are true and have the heart of You. Thank you that I can test every spirit by the spirit according to Your Word. Heavenly Father, I ask that You equip, protect, and give nourishment to Your people to fill them with Your word and not man. Father, I pray that You place a hedge of protection around them and send them the disciples to preach Your Word. Give them wisdom, knowledge, and understanding and the fruit of the spirit, O GOD, in Jesus's name I pray. Amen, Amen, and Amen.

Romans 12:8 NKJV He who exhorts, in exhortation; he who gives, with liberality; he who leads, with diligence; he who shows mercy, with cheerfulness.

INSIGHT

Dear Heavenly Father, thank you for another day to praise Your amazing name. I have another day to give You all the honor and glory, Father. I thank you for choosing me to be Yours. I thank you for changing me to be more and more like You every day. Thank you for making all things work in my favor. Lord, I ask You to release Your anointing power to bring me into your glory and feel Your holy presence and to commune with You. Lord, remove any emotions, feelings, or worries from this day and forever more, replacing them with your peace, Love, comfort, and your Holy Ghost power that destroy all yokes. Father, pull the scales off of my eyes and allow me to see into what You want me to see. I give You praise and glory in Jesus's name, I pray. Amen, Amen, and Amen.

Proverbs 8:14 NKJV Counsel is mine, and sound wisdom; I am understanding; I have strength.

REVELATION

Dear Heavenly Father,

I come and kneel down before You with a heart of praise and gratitude, giving You all of me. Lord, I ask that You bring forth Your power with revelation of what You want me to know. Lord, I cannot move without Your permission to do so. I come seeking You with my whole heart. Prepare my mind, body, and soul for what'is to come and all You have me to do. I thank you in advance in JESUS's name, I pray. Amen.

Revelation 21:5 NKJV Then He who sat on the throne said," Behold, I make all things new." And He said to me," Write, for these words are true and faithful."

HEARING

Dear Heavenly Father,

I thank you for loving and taking great care of me, calling me into Your marvelous light. Father, I ask that You anoint me to do Your will and strengthen me in every area of my life. I thank you for my body, which is Your holy temple. Lord God remove the old things, ways, and words in anything that does not bring glory and honor to Your name. Father, I want to thank you for opening my ears to hear You. Father God, I ask You to speak so I can get direct instructions and understanding of what You're saying in this hour and to order my steps in Your Word. Lord, allow me to continue to be the salt of the earth, which you have called me to help others to encourage, bless, and uplift in prayer with effectiveness. I thank you, Lord, because I know it is already done in Jesus's name. Amen, Amen, and Amen.

FOOD

Dear Lord Jesus,

I thank you for Your bread of life that nour-ishes me from the inside out and thank you for every word that is true and just. Thank you, Lord, for allowing me to sit at Your fine, glorious table, filled with goodness and mercy. Father allow me only to eat what is best for me, as I give praise and glory to You in Jesus's name I pray. Amen and Amen.

Matthew 4:4 NKJV B*ut he answered and said, "It is written, man shall not live by bread alone, but by every word that proceeds from the mouth of God."*

EMOTIONS

Dear Heavenly Father,

I thank you for life that is everlasting. Lord, I know sometimes I get emotional over things that makes me feel down. Father, give me the wisdom and strength to not walk in offence and not to become angry and bitter. I ask that You guard my heart and continue to do the work that You started in me. O Lord, let me always have the solutions in all things and not be moved by emotions, for You are bigger than anything. O God, I ask that You teach me, mold me, and impart into me Your spirit so I can do the right things first. Father, allow me to change the things that I can and to accept the ones that I cannot. You made me whole and complete, and I shall walk into all that You have for me. Let every assignment be fulfilled and allow me to be a blessing to others in Jesus's mighty name, I pray; and I thank you, Lord, in advance. Amen, Amen, and Amen.

1 Peter 5:7 NKJV Casting all your care upon Him; for He cares for you.

Psalm 23 NKJV

The Lord is my Shepherd; I shall not want. He makes me to lie down in green pastures; He leads me beside the still waters. He restores my soul; He leads me in the path of righteousness For His name's sake. Yea, though I walk through the valley of the shadow of death, I will fear no evil; For you are with me; Your rod and Your staff they comfort me. You prepare a table before me in the presence of my enemies: You anoint my head with oil; My cup runs over. Surely goodness and mercy shall follow me All the days of my life; And I will dwell in the house of the Lord Forever.

PROTECTION

Isaiah 54:17 NKJV No weapon formed against you shall prosper, And every tongue which rises against you in judgment you shall condemn. This is the heritage of the servants of the Lord, and their righteousness is from me." says the Lord.

Dear Heavenly Father,

I thank you for Your hedge of protection that covers my family and me, and all of Your children. Thank you for keeping us safe from all harm, hurt, and danger. I want to thank you for allowing the angels to minister and war on our behalf, in Jesus's name I pray. Amen, Amen, and Amen.

MIND OF CHRIST

Dear Heavenly Father,

I thank you for Your will to have the mind of Christ. I ask that You remove and cleanse my mind of any thoughts of the enemy. I thank you for the full armor of GOD that covers, shields, and protects me at all times. I thank you for creating me for greatness and with Your purpose to be fulfilled and to glorify You. I ask that You continue to always renew my mind. Give me all Your ways, O GOD, in Jesus's name I pray. Amen, Amen, and Amen.

Roman 12:2 NKJV And do not be conformed to this world, but be transformed by the renewing of your mind, that You may prove what is that good, and acceptable and perfect, will of God.

BREAKTHROUGHS

Dear Lord,

I come humbly to You with praise and thanksgiving. Lord, you have given me more than I
deserve or could even ask for. Lord, you are
good, and Your mercy endures forever. Father,
I come to You asking for forgiveness of my sins
and to lead me into all truth. Lord, I need a
MAJOR BREAKTHROUGH that will change my
entire life. I need You to open up the windows
of heaven and pour out the blessings that I will
not have enough room to receive. Lord, I ask
that You move in a mighty way to all that will
witness this and they will know this is a mighty
power move of JESUS CHRIST. Father, I ask
that You allow me to make room to receive
in JESUS's name, I pray. AMEN. IT IS DONE!

*Isaiah 43:19 NKJV Behold, I will do a new thing;
Now it shall spring forth; Shall You not know it?
I will even make a road in the wilderness, and
rivers in the desert.*

OBSTACLES

Heavenly Father,

I thank you for this day that You have made, for Your Word says that I shall rejoice and be glad in it. Lord, I ask that You keep me in the palms of your hands for eternal safety. Lord, I ask that You give me faith and take me from glory to glory to see the manifestations of Your unfailing Word. Lord, You said if I have the faith of a mustard seed that I can say to this mountain, "Move from here to there," and it will move. Nothing shall be impossible for You. I declare and decree that every mountain is moved in JESUS's name, I pray. AMEN.

John 16:33 NKJV These things I have spoken to you, that in Me you may have peace. In the world you will have tribulation; But be of good cheer, I have overcome the world.

MY BODY

Dear Lord,

I want to thank you for allowing me to wake up this morning to witness life that You have granted me here on earth. I give You honor and praise JESUS, for there is no one like You. I thank you for my body, which is Your holy temple and not of my own. I speak to my body that what is not of You cannot enter in; and if there is anything that needs to be removed, Father, take it out now in JESUS's name, I pray. AMEN.

1 Corinthians 6:19-20 NKJV

Or do you not know that your body is the temple of the Holy Spirit who is in you, whom you have from God, and you are not your own? For you were brought at a price: therefore, glorify God in your body and in your spirit, which are God's.

WORK

Dear Jesus,

I want to say thank you for my life and how You created me in Your image. I want to thank you for the spiritual gifts and talents and ask that You allow me to bless others that I encounter to always glorify You. Lord, I ask that You lead me to the right corporation that has Your principles in mind and who honor You and have love for Your people. I pray that we will come together in unity and bless Your holy name. Lord, I left my hands up to do my work unto you, in JESUS's name, I pray. AMEN.

Colossians 3:23 NKJV And whatever you do, do it heartily, as to the Lord and not to men.

VICTORY

HALLELUJAH! HALLELUJAH! HALLELUJAH!

Heavenly Father,

I want to give You honor and praise, lifting the highest praise, which is HALLELUJAH! The earth is yours and the fullness thereof. I want to thank you for laying down Your life so that I can live in You forever, and nothing can separate me from You. Father God, thank you for defeating the enemy, for the battle was already won by You. I THANK YOU FOR THE VICTORY IN EVERY CIRCUMSTANCE. Thank you for giving me the full armor of You and teaching, molding, building, and equipping me for Your magnificent glory. I want to thank you for exposing the lies, snares, and schemes of the enemy and giving me total victory according to Your Word (Jer. 13:26). Lord, I thank you for the victory banner You have placed over my life, in JESUS's name I pray. Amen, A men, and Amen.

Deuteronomy 20:4 NKJV For the Lord your God is He who goes with you, to fight for you against your enemies, to save you.

1 Corinthians 15:57 NKJV But thanks be to God, who gives us the victory through our Lord Jesus Christ.